A Traveler's Accolades

A Traveler's Accolades

Jason D. Evans

Copyright © 2009 by Jason D. Evans.

Library of Congress Control Number: 2009906812
ISBN: Hardcover   978-1-4415-5312-6
           Softcover   978-1-4415-5311-9

All rights reserved. No part of this book may be reproduced or transmitted in any form or by any means, electronic or mechanical, including photocopying, recording, or by any information storage and retrieval system, without permission in writing from the copyright owner.

This book was printed in the United States of America.

To order additional copies of this book, contact:
Xlibris Corporation
1-888-795-4274
www.Xlibris.com
Orders@Xlibris.com
65763

Contents

The Introduction 13

Omega's Prelude 15

From Day One 16

Preschool, Christian Academy to Be Specific 17

Adventures in the City with Father 18

Nice Hotels, Traveling, Father, Mother 19

Childhood Nightmares 20

Little Brother's Arrival 21

And Then There Was the Game Console 22

The School outside the City 24

In the Streets We Play 26

Uncertain Justice 27

Focus 28

Rainy Days to Wonder 29

Moments of Worth 30

Insatiable Rogues 31

A Solemn Plea while in Anarchy 33

Happy Birthday, Monica, My Love 36

I Hope, Sooner then Later 38

What Lies into Morrow . . . ? 39

A Snake's Poisonous Vision 40

Mind and Instinct	42
Black Stars	44
Agitated Mama	46
A Dark Glow	47
Another World	49
A Dark Journey Bright	50
Day of Departure	52
A Day in the Shoes of a Sailor	54
Colorful Boats	57
On the Fly, the Moon Creates Light, Thought Induced by Darkness	59
Love, Then Lost	60
What a Boat's Boredom May Produce	62
ATFP Hustle	65
Oceania	66
Beauty at Home, Alas, I Am Away	67
A Light in the Night's Sea	69
In Africa, I Found Myself, an Emerald Shellback	70
To Adventure	72
To Unique Adventures and New Beginnings	74
A Deadly Infection	77
How I Left, Unforgettable	79
Wetlands	80
Almost Fallen	82
My Love Confined	83
Lust Unquenched	84
During Absence	85
Gold For Blood	86

Poetic Brainstorm	87
Sailors' Breeze	88
From a Daughter's Dad	89
A Feeling So Old Is New	91
Look Deeper	93
A Sight to Behold	94
A Coastie's Ambition	95
Elusive Memento	97
Finding Favor	99
Young Moments	101
Legacy Once Lost	102
Beloved Brother	103
Behold, The Power of My Mother's Love	105
Grand Mother, Warrior	107
From Shadows to Spring	110
Book Summary	113
Author Biography	115

Dedication:

I dedicate this book to my mother
Monoka Lynn Collins
The greatest contributing factor
To all I have written
And have yet to write
May your legacy last forever.

In these poems contain,
All the things in life I've found
And though through darkness
Beauty bound...

The Introduction

Many, many chapters to write. Must not stop. These chapters are the story of my life. Are they great? Are they pathetic? Only I can be the judge of that. But, am I even judging? What am I doing? This story is beginning to tell too much of what I do not want to hear. Be silent, story! Why do you continue to speak? I cannot stop you, for this is my story. So I am in control? You must go on even it hurts me. I am talking to myself? I don't know, but I must go on because I am still alive. Right? I still have a chance to love, right? To find the true joy I seek. But what if I have found that joy!? How could I have been so foolish?! Who am I? Why do I see nothing in front of me? Is it because I do not want to? Is it because my eyes are closed? God, how foolish have I really been? How foolish am I still? Is it unnatural for me to wonder as I do? I must read to learn more. Books—yes, they hold the truth, don't they? Knowledge is power, right? But first, to read, I must stop wondering. I cannot!! Is it possible to do both? I am running out of lines. This story is fading? Where is my story going!? Don't go!! You mustn't go; you're all that I have left! My sanity, it has fled. My love was never present, friends lost to betrayal—I have nothing left. Only you. Even as I plead, I can sense your annoyance with me. So I myself shall depart. I am even more foolish than I thought; you know that I cannot leave! Not yet at least. What? You're not going? There's more!? Oh, thank heavens! Please tell me more! To be continued?!

Omega's Prelude

And so the passage has begun

From heaven to earth yet another son

Full of grace and dormant skill

On days very hot

Though also chill

So many gifts he'll eventually see

Manifest in him, majestically

And as colorful as a rainbow's birth

In the city of St. Louis

his newfound turf

So come along the adventures

And visions at random

This is his life's story

Or just versions in tandems

From Day One

A sea of church
Family members with love
Since before birth I heard them
Scriptures of great Kings and Queens
Prophets turned evil
Heroes of Old Legend
And then
In the light now still they continue
Tales of tremendous loss
And immortal victories
My family keeps strong these past times
The Good Book we call it
For strength in times of woe
In sickness and in Health
Go with God
Said my grandmother

Preschool, Christian Academy to Be Specific

A church and a preschool combined together
One could mistakenly think this place a Catholic school
I can't say I know a lot of black Catholics
The playground was small but big back then
Inside were little chairs and tables for us little people
The smell of crayons and love
The teachers were strict yet solemn
Illustrations of our imaginings haunted the walls
During nap time the light in the hallway beckoned
Mischief never sleeps
A new excitement grips me as well as my comrades
Like marines in the trenches on the velvet carpet
We muscle our way under the mats to glory
Just a bit further, to Mother's sandwich in my backpack
To an ice-cold drink out of the fountain
But alas!
We are discovered by the sentinel!
Lashing across the hand with the ruler commence
Jesus watches overhead from the cross
Father forgives
Though I see no wrong
I feel only hunger
And that of thirst

Adventures in the City with Father

The nights were always young

I remember bright lights

Quaint restaurants

A subtle breeze as my father leads the way

He would teach me things

I can no longer recall

But the warmth from his words I remember well

The smile my youth would conjure

His protective grip around my hand

I was loved

He was proud

Nice Hotels, Traveling, Father, Mother

The stars

So many now

Not Like before

Might as well have been going to Mars

Was it Chicago or Kansas City?

Mother, Dad, and me

The three musketeers we'd be

Fast food, grassy knolls, and road snacks

Cannot forget those groggy walks into the gas station—

After a lifetime of sleeping in Mother's little Honda

One hundred miles, fifty, twenty-five, five

We've arrived!

Luxurious out fittings Bedazzle

Mother's taste prevails again

The pool, clear as it is cool

And the arcades, classic

Such a sweet-smelling environment

As the day recedes into night

The young prince sleeps

While the king and queen—

Explore their new palace

All is well

Childhood Nightmares

Tugged out of my dreams into another darkness.
Where art thou favorable sleep?
Come unto me, for I fear
Though now the shades are but shadows
They may, in a short time, become more
The figment I so very hate
Inside reality has now estate
To roam and dwell outside my mind
Into which a room is mine
No touch
Nor smell comes hither there
Only the thought of treacherous scare
My fear and tremble reaches its peak,
As around my bed I look to seek
That monstrous vision I do not doubt
Has come and bidden me to shout

Little Brother's Arrival

I was still a kid when he decided to show up

My parents thought jealousy from me—

Would accompany

Though no such feelings arisen

Only the longing to teach my new confidante

To share with him a lonely prince's treasures

Our imaginations

Together they would make for grander adventures

And softer falls

Time unfolds as would a seed into a tree

Slowly yet solemnly

We are . . .

More than best friends

Though not as close to God

We are blood

And Then There Was the Game Console

The console

Such an artificial revelation

Create my gateway into mystical enlightenments!

Life in the mind conjures such illusionary dead ends

The fantastical advances of tomorrow

Never today come

Sadness searches for release

But to beautiful blue skies?

To the sweet chirping of red robins?

Perhaps the comfort of gentle green grasses?

One should say not!

And thus, the world was transformed!

The box inhibitor psychotropic

Warmth, all but stolen by lack of sun

Alas, the skies are darkened

A musty smog engulfs the land

Oh! And how the green grasses—

Are now but blood and empty shells

The chirping of birds

Replaced by the whistling of bullets—

And that of sudden death

Cover slowly disintegrates as the mind drifts

Where one wants to be

I mean, who's to free?

I take a deep breath

That one is me

The School outside the City

Clouds obscure the sun as the child waits
Mother's eyes watch attentively inside the car
Mother knows best
The boy is alone upon the street's corner
Nice clothes, book bag, lunch pail, pencils and paper
How majestic the utensils were to the boy
Loyal aids in the struggle for knowledge
Moments drift into subtle imaginings... Ahoy!
A yellow bus with students-
thereby summoned now see
A black boy standing, indifferently
Small black faces dwell within
Now traveling there out, a city of sin
Wonder begins to possess many
While all such surroundings transition—
Mesmerizing the young dark travelers

More and More—

As the sidewalks straighten

And the houses, how they increasingly dazzle in design

Though nothing could prepare their brown eyes to see

A great mansion of a school, magnificently

Outside black realm

They saw there

The youth all gilded, moreover fair

A transformation in days would come

To obstruct the old kingdom from where he had come

Friends now few

Due to his slang on low

A great test awaits

What answers shall one show?

In the Streets We Play

Thoroughly sought all the designated familiars
Few yet trustworthy upon the day of play
Custom grounds chosen from around the way
The minds search for areas to hide from the sun
A challenge thereafter set to commence the fun
The Catalyst is chosen
More random than supreme
To sprint and catch the one thus seen
Or perhaps to freeze the fellow in place
There until another enters the space
An old oak tree symbolized the proximity of rest
Ten to fifteen seconds they had at best
Then off once again the little hearts race
To scramble for sanctuary—
Or victory's sweet taste

Uncertain Justice

Let this pencil be my sword and with fury will it ignite.

This path I walk is long and amongst its darkness will I give it light.

This journey I walk is perilous, with monsters and demon entities alike, they try to cloud my judgment, bringing me confusion and some initial fright. This fear I keep in check, for my love and faith will always endure; life is long and beautiful, and unto mine I wish to remain pure.

So with this sword I will slay them, hatred, betrayal, and doubt.

For my cause being always noble, I will let none live nor shout, cries of fear and pain, it's too late to ask for forgiveness, there is none here, only your dreadful face satin, that which I wish to extinguish.

Focus

A journal writing a day helps keep these poetic thoughts in my head away. Or perhaps not. While in times of inspiration I drain my crystal sphere of creativity. The trick I find is to figure out a way to strengthen its regenerative powers, increasing the potency of my gift upon paper dramatically. In doing this, I can then start to fine-tune and sharpen the blade, which is my gift. The sharper it is, the better it will be at penetrating the skull of my host. Then and only will he or she be able to understand what it is that I have written. To find the words I cannot say aloud and make others feel them as they are prescribed upon paper. This is my will. This is the fantasy inside my head that I wish to bring into the minds of others. I can do it. But it's going to take a lot. It's going to take me.

Rainy Days to Wonder

This is my story. I'm here on earth. That much to me is all that is clear. Well, that and the love I have for my Father God. Life, beautiful, yet very uncertain. Uncertain, for I am myself uncertain. To what though, I cannot say. I only know that I am uncertain. Perhaps it is of the future. I often wonder where my legs will take me someday. Whom else I might find along the way. Perhaps another friend. Perhaps another enemy. Perhaps both again. Maybe I'll find a lover. Maybe another betrayer. I wonder if someday I will find true joy. I wonder if I already have, and never stopped to think about it. I hope that I haven't. I wonder if someday I will forget about all of this. This present, which ever so slowly slips into my past. Maybe I don't have much of a future. I wonder if it is because I think that I may not. Hopefully I do. I wonder why. Why I wonder. About others. About myself. I bet that it is in our nature to wonder. To dream about nothing, and everything. But is it OK?

OK just to wonder? To wait for a thought, that we hope to find while wandering with our minds. A great thought that will perhaps help us to wonder more. But, only to wonder. That is all I wish to do. And so, on that rainy day. During the story of my life, I thought, here on earth, of what to wonder. And in the midst of it all, all I really wanted to do was to write. I wonder what that means?

Moments of Worth

Though my sorrow in truth is full of beauty
I wish still to shroud it in darkness
For such divinity is almost unbearable
The past conjures such horrors and yet
They like seeds grow into something—
more than their own disappointments
and manifestations of emotional turmoil;
The loss of a love
the betrayal of a friend
the disappearance of prized possessions;
I ask myself
how could these things bring me peace?
In those moments I only know madness and despair
As time proceeds, yes, they dissipate
But only to greet me again when I am most vulnerable
I say then, how can my shortcomings
My dreadful errors
give me serenity?!
I can think of nothing;
Only that they
like many other events and occurrences of worth
make me feel
most alive.

Insatiable Rogues

A tale of two began one day
Bright as the light that the sun would convey
To the earth in which we dwell now together
For a great purpose we ride on as a feather
In the gentle breeze and also the harsh from a storm
To bring to those who so-called live in the norm
The truth of being and the sufferings past
In the future, present, our so-called saviors who cast
On us the people who hold the truth to equality and balance
To a reality aloof, of the lies and slander they teach us to breed, as well as the hate
and violence in our mouths they so feed. To keep us down, our faces in the gutter
So that we may never ever love one another
And while our strength is sapped, only misfortune will guide us
Wallowing in fear as the devils inside us
Leading us to do all except good
Because our horrible misfortune tells us we should
Knowledge is power, though many have not
Two rogues of a feather will shatter this plot
And bestow upon this world, with beauty divine
The rightness of wrong and the love we must find
We'll save a few, which in time will turn to a lot
Like untold legends in past times so fought
For us to live and breathe today

For us who've forgotten, but two rogues come to say
You people out there, black, white, and Asian
Japanese, Hispanic, Jamaican, and Cajun
We face a problem that threatens our planet
It is ourselves in part that take it for granted
We refuse to listen and hate to love
We see only our desire that is shown from above
The capitalist tower which hath flown like a dove
Away from sight, but two Rogues know is fleeing
Its purpose wrong and concept defeating
The Rogues see the obstruction and so try to right
The darkness's abyss, into understanding light
Many won't listen but a few will follow
And that is what we need for tomorrow
That some should fight, if many will die
For the truth is suffering, content a lie
And so it came to pass, the legacy now born
In two lives, understanding had torn
From the path of the people who refuse to see
The end of the world coming close to thee
But two Rogues see it, and so their tasks shall show
The power to avoid it
And understanding to know

A Solemn Plea while in Anarchy

We the people hold the answers
to unfair issues that kill us like cancers
We are strangled by our own nation and are not free
We are continuously subjected to rights we cannot see
These rights attack us though they should not
they should protect us but they do not
Instead they deceive, kill, and steal
under the constitution's ill-found will
Manipulated so cunningly and even to this day
to feed upon its poor helpless prey
And what are we to think? The people with the power
who are told to be grateful for this milk though is sour
sapping our strength this milk does so well
to those who are fools and cannot tell
The difference between freedom and that new technique
to enslave a race that cannot think
Without even whipping us or laying a hand
on our precious bodies; but instead a fan
is placed in our direction, so that a breeze
blows in our faces and makes us sneeze
out our essence slowly but surely
so that on the outside we still appear purely

so that we cannot notice the changes taking place
around us on earth, which hath a smiling face
but speedily that face is turning into a frown
for those whose lives have been turned upside down
because of the beatings, the neglect and lies
because of the hidden truth it ties
because of the monopolies, its greed and dark will
that hath been fabricated on capital hill
it feeds us visions and spectacles to fancy
it feeds us tainted food so chancy
McDonald's, Burger King, and Jack in the Box
into which all our money so flocks
In return we gain satisfaction, or so it may seem
for those who are still alive and death does not deem
It's funny how these laws protect our lives
though a contradiction in it so often ties
like cigarette smoke in the flowing wind
a poison in our mouths that often tends
to influence others to join the crew
to die a lot, never a few
And herb, the substance that's never killed a soul
is deemed inadmissible, to jail we will go

If it is found on us, that thick heavenly glow
From the lighter to the grass, that cloud I'd often blow
to this capitalist, conservative, secular crew
that holds all the power when it is ours past due
I reject their will and refuse to believe
in a dull, suffocated life reprieved
Of the Satisfaction that should be ours guaranteed
instead of all the bullshit they give us to believe
to die, to suffer, to despair is what it does
in television images that grab us like gloves
They fill us in the prisons for some stupid cause
that would never hurt a soul but often because
of their hatred and despise for us the people
it causes them to do not bad but evil
evil that is captured in the will of the good
so that in our minds it tells us we should
to oppose all against its apocalyptic faith
to all those companies it will reward very great
Hastening the end those in power do well
for whom that have not, as far as I can tell
Hope we still have, but a challenge it will be
to keep the inevitable end, from coming close to thee

Happy Birthday, Monica, My Love

Your birthday's past but it's not too late
to say from me that it's been great
to know you in this realm thus far
while on our bikes and in a car
during the night and whilst the day
to journey in this world and play
to fight for freedom and social cause
for those souls suffering we must give pause
you taught me this, Monica, my love
to live my life as if a dove
I soar and soar but forget to see
this world in dire need of me
but as fate would have it, I ran into you
an elegant Hispanic vision on queue

to journey and fight but also to play
for we love each other and so should stay
together forever inside our minds
if not in reality, which my heart so pines
to hold you in my arms and kiss
your sweet cheeks, perhaps your lips
Happy birthday, Monica, let me stop
this poem of passion before I flop
out of position, that angelic flow
into that utter devious glow
I tend to convey in my rhyming schemes
inside my light a darkness gleams
so let me just say, so you will know
my love for you will always grow.

I Hope, Sooner then Later . . .

To later days, when the sky is darkened by lack of sun. To later days when the day that was lost is finally won. To later days, when my love finally appears. To later days when that benevolent dream of mine is real. On that day I will cherish most her eyes, her lips also for loving me so. To later days when such dreams don't bestow upon me such great woe. When I am alone, I understand those days that made me think of such a face. Those days wish have died for me, comforting the almost inescapable case. That case I know will one day be my end. It clouds my very soul and hurts me so. Inside this cloud constitutes all my sin. And only until my death will it flee. But my sin is what makes me love so dear! Such a love I know will make me free! This freedom I need more than anything, and it would be by grace that she, who would grant me this great favor, the wonderful privilege to love only me. This love I would cherish more than life itself, for that is what to die for. Love cannot be taken away, even after death, does it recycle. So I would tell her always of my great love for her, and the connection always she would see, love's bond is so great, and so in my eyes great she would always be. But, she is not there; there is no one, only me. I don't know who I am, and so I need such a love to tell me so. In later days, then and only, will I be able to grow, into that man I am meant to be, faith and valor strong! Only a woman's love can grant me this. This now I do not have. Only loneliness comforts me, to later days.

What Lies into Morrow . . . ?

A Disastrous blight seeks to find

My beauty in life which art divine

Shrouded with darkness

Dividing the light

Coursing through shadows in aerial flight

Searching for victims and souls such as I

To bring us ill will so in darkness we cry

But the heavens are far

Therefore faith must comfort us

To days untold in revelations of trust

I see that hour clearly when in dreams of the light

Though always the darkness tries to curse me with fright

It says there's no end to these moments of sorrow

Even in death will they last into morrow.

A Snake's Poisonous Vision

A reason for anger is always good

To quell the pain that burns like wood

The burning was wrong

So pain is right

After that snake and its venomous bite

Into the night it dives again

With its degenerate, devious kin

To rebel and laugh at what it's done

To the bastard child

To Christ, His son

So in the darkness I sit again

Cold as I was with fury then—

that I first received such a devilish blow

With those unrighteous fangs below

White was the snake as it fled into the night

Again and again with terror and fright

For I will not die

The burning is good

It strengthens my skins as iniquities should.
And as flames burn wood they increase my sight
Into that eternal glorious night
Allowing my texture
A little broader then brown
To understand nature
Safer then sound
I close my eyes and see it in flight
A precarious, glistening, luminous light
I rub my wounds
Thereafter returning my sight
My mind is now clear
I have control of my fight
It resonates in sin I shall not show
Till life in heaven I will one day go
Sooner than later
During these venomous bites
I murmur to myself
As I shudder in the night
Yes, I shall go afterlife
But until then I must live
In the forest of sorrows
And this vision it gives

Mind and Instinct

Nothing comes to mind as I sit here alone

Only my presence as I protest of its throne

My body is apart from my spirit within

Though always it craves the flesh of her skin

That one girl so fair

Or black as the night

I would fight so dearly for such brilliance in sight

And though I see in dreams

Moreover reality still

A creature of divinity

Captured on earth's heel

There's always another vessel

Or some desire of short worth

That I cannot supply

So my loneliness rebirths

Again and again

Like an infectious disease

That causes me to want no more than to cease

Those glimpses of beauty

Heaven on earth

Dreadful desire

Alas, its rebirth

Consuming me whole—
Lust does still today
That wanting of her
Unto my eyes so play
A fantasy's design
Away with you reason
Give me sweet passion
Always in season!
But that is my body
Not the spirit within
Who needs only peace
peace from this sin!
Sin is what corrupts!
My soul cries unto me
Stay away from it
Or so you shall see.
What you desire
Is an illusion of pain
For a moment it's good
But the rest of its shame

Black Stars

How could my beautiful black color

Come with such a curse

The hatred and animosity with its unquenchable thirst

For reasons unknown it seeks to steal my joy

And my passion to love and fight

In its devious evil ploy

Like a white ominous cloud it follows me

Here and there

To seek my destruction in every one of my affairs

It leads me to despair and wonder—

At its presence, for I am good and true

And to others held in high reverence

But to it I am dirty and evil because of my beautiful black skin

My full lips which love true

And the seeds that carry my kin

Be defeated! It says to me

Lie down and be still! Do as we command

And be humble, under our heel

But I say to it, No, with Might!

My faith and valor are strong!

I will put this curse to good use

It will be a powerful beacon, a song!

For those whom are like me

And face a pain to great to erase

My darkness will be a light to all in this same retarded case
This poem shall be a light, for the darkness that I am in place
When I walk and/or still in this horrible neglected place
My people let us stand together
For I am only one voice
This curse may be too great for me
So we have to make a choice
To be subdued or fight
With that great light in which we all possess
Inside the darkness of our skin
Let this curse only be a test
Of our resolve which is best
In these times of great opposition
Let us rise above those clouds
And the earth, into our correct position
Black Stars

Agitated Mama

What soul has become mine, but the one that wishes not to climb. From the struggles of the hard I have come, to bestow upon this world a son. But with all the faith and guidance I give, he still wishes not to be alone and live. I wonder what more I could share, of what great witness I could bare, to he whom I gave life, in this world of sin and strife. I wish for him to be away, so that I may have my own life and pray, in silence and in peace, with a great husband and cease this trial and error case, which is his life to live and waste. I want no more of his business, for I am tired, cold, and frigid. Give me an end, Lord, to this drama! of being his strong, independent mama, I've done all I can, I must say, it is now his burden to live and pray, for the long days into the future, let mama's past teachings suit ya.

A Dark Glow

With this talent I shall show
the power of God, the truth to know
each and every soul out there
who has a strength, an ominous flare
To reach above the clouds so high
into the heavens where angels fly
but not that soul who refuses to see
the end of the world coming close to thee
These we must save, those who see
The truth, our God, a thriving tree
A tree of mercy, glory strong
for whom are weak and right is wrong
for whom are tired, God has rest
from the wretched sinful mess
of this life we now possess
which is merely but a test

a test of self inside of us
to do all bad, but good we must
for that day in truth we know
will come to pass, and so will show
how we did on this blue earth
to the present, from our birth
your story's long but short to Him
and so a decision, in a whim
will decide your fate, heaven or hell
which eternal fate will fail?
I hope it is hell, but without God
Damnation will be your only façade
so change your ways, now you know
the darkness of hell
and a glorious glow.

Another World

As I close my eyes
Dreams profound
Sustain and reach a distant ground
Drawing a world familiar to me
Under the earth though before the sea
In the crust
Between the light
Lies a shadowy brownish night
Half's my skin
The rest my soul
Constantly plays a costly role
Dwelling within
Fate and chance
Dreams of chaos and life's romance
Inflict upon me a responsibility
A colorful art, for all to see
So till that end
I will fight
For that gorgeous, egregious night
Further and further
Away from the dark
For all who believe
To heaven we hark.

A Dark Journey Bright

In this dreary mood I feel
detached from life, no love appeals;
in the darkness of my skin
a light is shown
but sometimes dim
in the shadows of my heart
that often grows, but then apart
from the lights which now aren't bright
inside the shadows of the night
the night, my path, my soul, the light
barrels through the journey's blight
to seek and find the source, my Lord
so that this journey's gift affords
the pain and sufferings it's come to know
Its truthful purpose, in beauty show
its divine intentions, in lessons blow
the breath of God, an eternal flow
of love and gifts beyond this world

unconditioned truth, reality pearled
Life egregiously packaged fine, for one wise soul-
To whom is mine
So till that end my travels shall show
my traces of light, in beauty they glow
onward and onward journeying fast
the sinful night in courage pass
the lust and desire for this world
the understanding hindered
salvation hurled
across the mountains and the valleys
into the sky where heaven rallies
but not that soul who refuses to see
the end of the world coming close to thee
my home is heaven and so I shall show
dark times the difference
And how they glow.

Day of Departure

An epic journey lies ahead

Though in deep preparation

The mind wanders

Still it drifts to that one

Or perhaps many

Who will

After that reluctant day of departure

Become somewhat of a lucid dream

Like a phantom they haunt us

Their aroma

Their touch

That sweet, familiar kiss

Invokes tears

On gloomy, rainy days

How can a week become a year?

A month, eternity

The wind becomes their voice

Our mementos are now time machines

Madness begins to threaten reason

The sun

No longer does it shine

Nor does the sea soothe.

If only letters couldn't end

If only dreams were more real

Uncertainty constitutes self-loathing

Love into longing

Alas

what is life

without the other?

A Day in the Shoes of a Sailor

The light peers inside my rack
Yet another day to test my worth
Shower, sandals, ODU, boots
Sea legs give me speed
Twenty-nine seconds until muster
Groggy faces, clouds of sarcasms
Superiors enter, stage left
Orders the same
Only today's Tuesday I think
Forget the time, help it pass
My face conjures a bitter smile
Fifteen minutes until break
Boat-lowering details been set
My smile quickly dissipates
The past becomes present
Old friends, familiar places
Beloved family, cherished events

Mustn't lose focus
Though the past
Grants thee peaceful pause
A shipmate steps through the haze
He offers me watch
That which I cannot refuse
I become the ship
I become the sea
Commands come in revelations
Error always in solemn
The day's only half-over
Again my smile appears
Time for chow
Long lines, the number five
Wellness manifests reflection
While the sea provokes thought
The whistle howls

Twenty-five-cent coins
The gods dictate
The mortals assimilate
Red curtains obscure the stage
We gather in coteries
Later awaiting the incentive
It comes as a sourceless voice
And commands our labor
In a blur of action it ends
Ra surrenders unto Poseidon
The allure of darkness induces sleep
My rack is velvet
All is quiet
Home rocks the few awake into dreams
Sentries roam and watch like angels
The light peers inside my rack
Yet another day to test my worth

Colorful Boats

At any given day

There is a boat at sea

A ship, if you will

With great diversity

From all walks of life

They come to progress

And though sometimes

Their ideals conflict

They soon come to remember

That they are stuck together

The goals shipmates strive for

Are always one and the same

The boat's strengths

And weaknesses

Are intermingled with their lives

Language is the same

But past tales

Are what differentiate unto them

Inside each individual

Lies a story

Dying to be told
Shy perhaps at first
But always longing to be felt
These creatures come to understand
This ritual of speech is essential
Fear and repression
The usual barriers
Faith and trust
Always key
Operations and uncertainty
Never cease to test one's resolve
Ability and courage
Service voluntary
Compelled by some volition to fight
Serve and protect
Sailing . . .
At any given day
There is a boat at sea
A ship, if you will
With great diversity.

On the Fly, the Moon Creates Light, Thought Induced by Darkness

Alone

And yet hand in hand

One cradles the other

At times one is gentle

Though the next malicious

White pillars loom about

In the majestic wind manifested

shadows descend below

A mythical beast perhaps

Light transforms into darkness

And in turn the moon

Creates light yet again

A road appears in Poseidon's wake

Thrusting and crashing against itself

Many ignore the calling

But the invitation always stands

To whom do we decline this honor?

Love, Then Lost

Continuous dread unto light

The darkness bravely fought

Though wholly different is this plot

In those moments that pass

So full of love

As time recedes into the heavens above

Our gazes meet

This conjures our smile

No longer the darkness

Such anger so vile

The heart dares to hope

Neglecting all reason

Acting as though love has but come into season

Star-crossed lovers

Were we ever meant to be?

One must follow their path

But so faithfully?

Worlds collide

Together we see

One's colorful past so symmetrically

The day goes on
Well into the night
Strangers become friends
Perhaps more is in flight
One may never know
In fact such is this plot
Of a shirt not fully sewn
A sentence without its dot
I sit and write in question
Though the answer I will never know
Of a love I could have had
In a time now long ago

What a Boat's Boredom May Produce

The darkness harks unto the day
I never know during which to play
I sing and dance every now and then
But usually stop around the evening of ten
I'll go to my room where others lay
And wonder why it is I play
Clutching my chin, my eyes look high
Pouting my lips as if to cry
I try to analyze it as alien clay
Or the light on the sea
From the moon in a ray
Watching her sing and dance on the fly
The sun, the moon
The sea doesn't lie
A boat she rocks quite far and fair
While others wonder seeing her there
And I on her
Wondering why
It is on the boat that others cry

Even myself
I mean who could see?
The evil manifested inside of thee
Towards others
Not love
Instead of which
Should beat in our hearts
As would a switch
Though what's real is sad
For love is rare
On the road of hurt
Was it left there...?
Alone we make the boat a temple
To conjure stress as if it were simple
Shrouded by darkness
How thy dwells with the night
But during it won't thou burn so bright?
Keep the hurt
Only makes thee strong

The wisest paths thy walk alone
And always should you help your mate
Even if they manifest you hate
See through the darkness
From inside the light
Which we all together
Must journey and fight
My wanderings complete
I now lie to rest
For with each coming day
Lies a new cunning test

ATFP Hustle

The world's on our shoulders
It feels from the vest
And M16 across the chest
Though strangely enough
It becomes that clear
As we gaze from far to near
Seeking those that wish to harm
All the good we would perform
A family tree of might we be
From the past to save all thee
The rivers rage
And as hurricanes howl
We step in the mist
A humble bow
Proceeds the rescue
That extinguishes fear
Our aim is true
As the tactical gear
We wear on days as hell may know
The bow and stern back to and fro
Thinking how now
It's become so clear
The enemy in sight
Oh death is near

Oceania

Strange

that the wind should come from the sea

And what's more, my heart should fall for it

Gazing forth, I lose focus on what's there

And begin to see what my heart desires

Silence, lonely heart!

As if having a mouth to speak, my heart preaches to me

Would that you should leave your mother, family, and friends!

And for whom?! Oceania

the Dark Mistress who does not speak

Who cares nothing for you! She is an Ancient murderer

A shadow of lost secrets, a bitter sea of sorrows!

But, though merciless, 'tis true that

In the nature of all things, she is fair.

Without the sacrifice she forces, how can legends be born?

And though she taunts my mind with visions of faithful past

Is the past not what I long for the most?

Precious moments in truth can never be forgotten.

Continue to conjure my hopes, dreams, and that of others

Moreover, my biggest failures and my greatest triumphs

Give me new tales, that of adventure, that of tears

Weariness and blood forged into something more

Something fit for legend

Like you, Oceania

Beauty at Home, Alas, I Am Away

On a boat I sit and think
To chain events so that they sync
Into this one that is so fair
Slightly tanned and dark of hair
Those lips so sweet
And eyes as brown
Angelic is that voice of sound
It takes me to this place I know
Full of peace and heartfelt flow
I conjure words inside of thee
Now opened wide the darkness free
In my soul once shadows possessed
All that's good and would be best
Only now it's come to pass
The darkened plot no sinful last
Shattered by song
So graceful is she
That has come to restore what once couldn't be

In thy eyes she seemed a dream
If my senses weren't so keen
They tell me, self
You are in love
With this wondrous graceful dove
So from you, dark knight
I shall depart
Said my fleeting, lonely heart
And off it walked
Perhaps to stay
Through years and years of night and day
I wished my heart well
Though it's now hers
To which this poem of reflection refers

A Light in the Night's Sea

Suffice to say

We ought to cry

But instead we death defy

During the trials that lie ahead

Never before seen

Await us dread...

Murky seas full of light

Whilst the day

And moon at night

Alone at sea so often bare

When times are rough

No loved ones there

A familiar darkness consumes the light

But during it won't though still burn bright?

Conjuring methods inside of thee

Skill and cunning for all to see

Thankful we are

The source now found

Truth in darkness

Such beauty profound

In Africa, I Found Myself, an Emerald Shellback

The shades flow past
Alone silent night
A bright shell emerald
Flows ahead right in sight
The left goes away
So forward with might
Over past failures
Regrets constant fight
King Neptune awaits
And beside him, his queen
At the end of the gauntlet
Clouds open, a beam
Descends from the heavens
Unto the sea gentle love
Be calm harsh mistress

As Christmas tree doves
And then . . .
A rock is crushed
Perhaps nothing is left
Uncertain as the sea
Of its weight and/or depth
But a diamond is there
I mean, who could have thought?
That at the end of a journey
Lies another forged plot.

Jason D. Evans

To Adventure

A wonderful tale of adventure awaits
Though now in the past which future creates
Each other we'll need
On this journey we travel
Into the void of the sea's lonely battle
A task unlike others
Stands in our stead
Off into the sea
To Africa we tread
The ocean is magnificent
Such beauty divine
Cherished are moments we see it and find
Now our world is behind us
And as the blue one awaits
So do the jobs that lie for each rate
Security, training, and maritime our focus
Unveiling to foreigners as would a large Nymphaea lotus

Cape Verde was first

Up to Gabon we'd head next

Helping their military to become the very best

The languages would change

But our mission would not

With each port we'd hit

So would another forged plot

Whether it be helping the locals in COMREL projects

Or scoring a goal in their soccer game's nets

We'd be there, the Crew!

And the Dallas, our comfy nest

Supporting the nations and passing their tests

Camaraderie the ticket

Countless Cultures the guests

A gorgeous Waltz we'll show them

Our excellence no less.

To Unique Adventures and New Beginnings

The day had finally come
No more in dreams
And as the family waves good-bye
The car waits patiently
Luggage packed, bills auto, snacks secured
Cigs sat, music favorites, movies, and games . . .
Something is forgotten, no matter . . .
Oh, how the pier will be missed!
The walk to her on that day—
It seemed longer than the others
Our new mother, waiting humbly
As we, like children, mustered to her bosom
Dallas, you are a sight to behold
Slow and yet swift
Towards the open seas again
Farewell, familiars
God willing, I shall return
Hello, Poseidon

Never do you change
Though your obstacles are quite clever
We endure
New bonds form within us during each trial
With each emergency, we are made stronger
For what else is to come?
One can never be certain
The tides recede upon Africa
Blessed be the Lord
We have arrived!
An unfamiliar heat torments us
The locals appear cool
As if under a tree of shade
We puzzle one another
For our languages
Body and speech differentiate
But the mission is one
Security for the Nation
Training for those who fight for justice
The tools to combat struggle

Mighty Dallas, she has come to help!
Liberty, Liberty, Liberty!
Such times call for exploration
Worlds of beauty and sorrow obscure stereotypes
As strangers become friends
Language barriers break
And hearts become one
Customs as well as tradition manifest in merchandise
To the people
We are walking mementos
Of a land and lifestyle sought by so many
News cameras train themselves on us
Ambassadors and other diplomats show support
Under the tent of Dallas we toast
To new beginnings

A Deadly Infection

There exists something so precious
In this world we must find
A sensation as old as the ancient time
And as elusive as the wind
In which carried It from there
Married with God for the people to share
But often we do not
Carry this with thine
So that in another we'd enjoy its shine
'Tis a figment we provide
Just a drop of lust
To that brief feeling
How we reach to clutch
But it's not there . . .
What is it we had?

That felt so good
So good was bad
And how bad left us!
To this awful plot
'Tis strange why things exist
To one day be shot
And yet we're alive
Or shall I say the walking dead
Those in whom lost love
Yet love is not dead

How I Left, Unforgettable

What is it that I have
Which before I could not know
Like the slushy mess
After the pure white snow
Such moments of perfect harmony
Were those days I left in the past
Now but figments of family and friends
As if forever they would last
Though soon enough they end
Those times now long ago
The darkness how it easily swallows
All the light I burn to show
And how life changes so suddenly
As the seasons and growing pains
Glistening in the day so brilliantly
Until at night it morphs to **shame**
A monster lurking amongst the shadows
Consuming hope and reason
Restlessly stalking me as I travel
Towards a future of war and treason

Jason D. Evans

Wetlands

Left from home
Right to sea
Away from those
Loved by thee
Families far
Yet all around
Place thy feet
On solid ground
Foreign lands
Eyes now see
Manifested variety
Inspired to be
Conscious life
Inside of time

Rhythmic flow
Ruby shine
Meditated greatness
Ahead at sea
Always close
Yet far from thee
Give those hope
Merciful light
Let it shine in corners
Where dark is so bright
And after that time
Allow them to see
Their loved ones at home
Where they'd ought to be.

Almost Fallen

There he lay
As if to ponder
Shifting thoughts and wallowing wonder
Protrude from his mind during the dead of night
Such roads less traveled seem full of fright
This he says out loud while there
His eyes now closed in darkness bare
The room seeming quiet
Though the voices still come
During thoughts of hate yet heaven's full sum
On gloom-covered days
While the pain tastes sweet
Of betrayal, the lies, and people who cheat
Those all seem close
But to a clever man far
Like the destruction of a dream
Of a cliff in a car

My Love Confined

Inside my pain, I search to find
The beauty in it which is divine
The marvelous wonders
Which off doves would climb
Roses, sunflowers, and the ancient time
Deeper and harder I must search for thine
For thy precious presents off the heavens should chime
Plums, kisses, and strawberries galore
My love for her, how it wishes to soar!
But I say to it no
And reluctantly so
That she loves not us
And wishes for love to go
To the confines of this poem
I command my love to stay
For the beauty of her
I hope, wish and pray
Perhaps someday she will want me
But today she does not
So my love in this poem
Must stay for this plot
Until that righteous day
When you may see another shot
I say to you, love, stay
Till that day be your lot.

Lust Unquenched

Sensations of strangled desire
Please rest in peace
Sinful allure
Favor and strength be mine
Through isles of loneliness
Flow over me like the ocean's current
When the sensation of my lustful desire unfolds
The epic battle against temptation begins
And when the smoke clears from the fight
My true love will manifest
Like the pleasant dream
After a long slumber

During Absence

The darkness eventually washes over the raging sun

Voiding the things in its light would come

And how the earth is shadowed

Creating an absence of sight

Which to some, perhaps many, is a tremendous delight

Or as our mind slowly conjures an unseen form

The darkness manifests a fear made of scorn

To those that are sensitive to the spiritual realm

Or to the unknown

which no one can tell

Gold For Blood

Shrouded by darkness
I trudge through a shadow
Seeking remembrance of beauty in battle
Forged in red
Shrouded by black
A light to find glory
His hint of the fact
Secures my fate
That in time will be sealed
But to Him in whom a sinner is healed
I must remember
As I ponder in stealth
Remember His forgiveness
And promise of wealth
This sickening earth is all but a test
For me to endure and rise as the best
I shall conquer desire
From heaven on earth
For Righteousness is
The Final rebirth

Poetic Brainstorm

Clouds, Plums, familiar faces, Life streams, melancholy sufficed, Unforeseen grace, distant hearts, dark energy quelled, smell of essence, eyes as bottomless wells, setting suns, seas haunted now holy, true feelings hidden, heaven harked, God near, souls astray

zero out for now today.

Jason D. Evans

Sailors' Breeze

Praised by the gods
Ye art worthy
Laid to rest
But not before the drink
Again familiar faces
Cheeks redder then usual
We are bards!
Our tales
Days, months, now years old
Are legend
As the wind whispers
To those who might listen
Together we fellowship in dreams
As light peers inside thy rack
As drills surface
Only to recede
Again and again
All eyes steady
Commands, actions, and emotions
Ready
Semper Paratus

From a Daughter's Dad

Since your dawning day
You've been in my heart
A mixture of sweetness
Beauty as art
Nothing's more important than you are to me
I would do anything on earth just to see
Your little smile grow
Or to hear your laughter
'Tis the greatest joy
But what's more is after
Some time on earth
You will begin to grow
And I can watch with pride and know
You once were a precious girl
Which in you I'll always see
Like the timeless love I've bestowed upon thee
So you'd be happy
But also strong
For life is good
Though sometimes wrong

Before you were born I learned to see
When God had given a gift to me
And so with my goodness
I shall pay the fee
For you are all that's right in thee
Whether it be ponies, puppies or toys
One cannot put a price on the amount of joy
That you've given to me, my sweet little fair
To bring you pleasure is all that I care
Like to see your smile
Or to hear your laughter
Is all I really want thereafter

A Feeling So Old Is New

I'm beside myself with passion
But I mustn't let anyone know
The love in thee I wish to show
I hold my tongue
And dare not touch
Though in me I want so much
These dreams they come
Many thoughts I fancy
That includes such desires
And risks so chancy
I fill my mind
With sound and wonder
Blades of grass
More visions of thunder
Continue to strike
My beating heart
Which cries for you
To heaven I hark
Please give me peace!
I hurt from laughter
And the care for her thereafter
The warmth in my heart
This continues to glow
Brighter and brighter

Unto her I'll let know
That once there was
A lonely lad
His poetry solemn
This made him glad
He'd write compelling stories
So others could read
Granting him the glory
And perhaps an inspiration's seed
But no one really cared that much
Of his words upon which to touch
Though one day in the clearing there
Came a lady beauty rare
She read his poems
From inside his file
And as she did, it made him smile
He wishes to say so much to her
Of his love he would refer
But he cannot
This hurts him so much
Maybe in this poem
Their hearts will touch.

Look Deeper

Let not your heart be heavy
All things shall be made new
Like love at first sight
Or a good song after its queue
Peace can be found
In sickness as well as health
The time now is for hope,
Meditation, pray and understand
For He who resides in heaven
He has a righteous plan
A perfect design
Faith is the bridge
An invitation to bliss and true understanding
Cross it, friend
And watch
As all things are made new.

A Sight to Behold

Mountains of turmoil

Trees with torrent riot off cold valleys

Ordaining the crisp winter air

Shrouded in darkness

Some seek serenity in the Obscurity

Repetition breeds destruction

Storms create fire

The warmth detours anxiety

And dusk, harmony.

Rustle through the leaves, oh wind!

Manifest thy peace if only for a moment

The sky blue pierces the clouds for an instant

A young fellow in the clear raises his arms in reverence;

Aren't thou connected to all

The clouds, the precipitation

The sun, even over such great distances?

Rupture the earth, oh powerful quake!

Twist with valor, my typhoon!

Churn the sea and seek serenity, sweet eye of the storm!

That all should be a part of such beautiful contradictions of gentle nature

'Tis truly the greatest gift!

A Coastie's Ambition

With His Grace

We'll sail the sea

Though coursing towards uncertainty

Through thunderous storms

And howling gales

To save a life we shall not fail

It is our lot

To guard the sea

Though blood sweat and pains the fee

In thy heart exists courage strong

Through raging rivers

And the ocean's song

Our vision is clear

But the sea is a mist

It clouds our vision

And slackens our fist
So we most remember
His mercy divine
To strengthen our will
Like an emerald shines
In life we may die
So that with honor we will live
Inside the heart of another
Whom we've pledged our life to give
In Davy Jones's locker
Our souls will sail free
We are the righteous who die willing
To save a life
Or take from thee

Elusive Memento

Waiting seems to be all I do
My gears they shift as if on queue
Anticipating the moment that I'll be free
To the skies I'll take so far from thee
I worship the blue while I sit eyes closed
Falling through the clouds as no one knows
And as reality waits just a blink away
I conjure a pray to myself and say,
Oh angels, as I drift in the atmosphere
No one to hate—
Or hate to fear
Their are glimpses of the darkness I see in the light
And while I witness an evil to fight
He sends his minions to possess humans on earth
Ignorant as a fetus while it rests before birth

Plotting countless ways on how to strike me down
Like how sadness dissipates
From the face of a clown.
Meditation induces inside my mind;
I reach . . .
And in doing so even more unwind
But the skies begin to lessen
As reality calls me back
Only now seconds left of serenity
One of the few matters of fact
So please manifest yourselves
Old angels of war
Battle my demons
To the heavens I implore.

Finding Favor

Clouded visions and heartfelt ends
Oceans of sorrows seek to mend
That which was lost on those timeless days
With those so cherished in childish ways
Thy colors so bold now attempt to part
From inside a single precious heart
Manifested grandeur
Primed in gold
Red and violet
Thy silver so bold
Chasing each other
How they blend in ways
Never thought before
As a calculated maze
Searching frantically for a source of light
The darkness ever present
How passionately they fight
Abstract and yet focused
One watches to see
The visions of beauty
Conjured in thee

So many questions now constitute the mind
As one peers inside such beauty divine
Never really sure
If from this realm or the next
Only to watch
And hope for the best.

Young Moments

The day had been long
Like many more to come
Not to worry though
The river's water is cool now
The feeling steals our hardships
And replaces them with awe
If only for a moment;
Surrounded by kindred
All is well
As the gentle breeze whispers
Sweet nothingness in our ears
As the sun's pure light
Reflects off the water so clear
The mind drifts
To those loved ones far away
Gazing at the boats
While back and forth they sway
Together on the pier we sit
As we share old stories
And laugh without regard
Of what lies ahead

Legacy Once Lost

On this night I'll start anew
Before the past obscures my view
Of all the ones I love the most
In this poem to them I'll toast
Even the ones who've done me wrong
Because of them I am now strong
The will to fight I have in thee
And all the hurt I once could see
Though now I see that without pain
I would in fact now be the same
Not the one whom now has might
Courage for the dead of night
While consumed in darkness
I choose to fight
With that glorious flame so bright
To overcome thy circumstance
I am the victor, and not by chance

Beloved Brother

At times it takes all of thee
to open wide the darkness free
And, not like the moments
In the past I implore
when the light was pure
forevermore
when we were together
to share the pain
of despair, fear and other shame
It is now so different
how our lives have become
we are now like neo
who is "The One"
and who'd would have thought?
you and me
would travel so far away from thee
It saddens my heart
though makes me glad
that we've found success
in this life we've had

but its not the same

without my lil bro

when in the past we'd explore

both to and fro

and yet it is the same

but now were apart

I mean in real life

your still in my heart.

Behold, The Power of My Mother's Love

I feel my mother's love
When I create my works…
For this poem is her
Though the voice is me
Who begs and pleads to be set free
To the gentlest woman
I love the most
Yes, to the fieriest fighter
To her I'll toast!
Now…
I wish to tell a story
Though it is still far from over
This story is of a woman
Whose love gives luck like a clover
The woman I speak of is my Mother
Who teaches me to give nothing but my best
Such radiance she bestows upon me
Allows my soul never the less
I have watched her as she has fought

So very hard for me and my brother
Through the day and whilst the night
As we've rested soundly undercover
My mother fights without reserve
With a boundless love and infinite conviction
The power of her inspiration
Is so awesome it sounds like fiction
With this great strength she raised to boys
And twas with all her love she gave to them
So that they might glow inside this world
Like an emerald or exquisite gem
We will be her mark upon this earth
When far in the future my mother is gone
Though stays this poem
An immortal memory
Like the lasting impression of a song

Grand Mother, Warrior

From my birth

You were there to see

A benevolent beauty manifest in me

You cared for me

As my Mother would

When times were tragic

But also good

And with your love

You nurtured my light

For you knew the darkness would seek so to fight

You've bestowed upon me the goodness of God

So with me I carry a heavenly facade

And you've given my mother strength

Which in turn she gives me

And perhaps one day my children

If God's will is to be.

Your great Grandmother's the greatest!

I'll tell them as God's will is

Her love could encompass the world
But instead it's all yours, yes it tis!
And love can survive the most terrible storm
While created in ruin and breathed through scorn
On our Earth unrighteous
Most clever at best
Though this is but God's unruly test;
For love will endure
Though at times I thought not
For what could I do against darkness's plot?
I used to think myself such a pitiful soul
Who could not create light
If ever I had coal
But inside my shadow
There always came light
From the source I'd see Grandmother in sight!
She'd smile at me and tell me to fight!
While I basted in the warmth of her awesome white light
Courage and wisdom she always gives thee

From the love of God so individually;
My journey's been long
But so much lies to travel
And with it I'll carry her history of battle;
My Grandmother's a Warrior!
And so shall I be
To the kingdom of God
We will both one day see.

From Shadows to Spring

And so the journey ends
Yet others await our travel
New paths hopefully soft
Though perhaps made of gravel
The path I walk is such
Sadly trudging towards despair
My life is but a shadow
A perfect devil, without a care
And though I chase the elusive light
The darkness stains in envious blight
Obscuring all roads bidden to me
Now treacherous thy fate
How cursed it be.
But, during the endless lonely nights
I found the will to stand and fight
Far off I see the clearing there
Outside the darkness beauty fair
Sharing wholesome lovely light
Grassy plains and doves of flight
Sky's so blue
So blue 'tis bright!
My God, its heaven!
Though in mine sight
Apart from darkness standing bare

While I wonder seeing it there
Now the devil wondering why
I choose to run as if to fly
Coursing for that burning light
That gives thee strength to brave my plight
Inside my darkness
Yet far from me
I feel the eyes that wait to see
If I'll fail and cease to travel
On this blackened road of gravel
Towards that awesome, glorious light
That now and then goes out of sight

Book Summary

I started writing poetry when I was in high school as a means to understand my feelings more deeply. Inside my mind chaos and yet also beauty exist. This creates countless questions and yet sometimes answers to the endless possibilities inside my reality. These occurrences seemingly war with one another. I write to make sense of these battles and find true beauty. Over the years I've sought to cultivate this method, nurture it, so that not only might I be able to understand and learn from it, but others may as well. This book is my first attempt, I hope it's worked.

Author Biography

I was born in the city of St. Louis and later on down the road I joined the Coast Guard. A lot of interesting things have taken place since I've been on Earth. Over the years those interesting things have become a great part of who I am today. We are an embodiment of all the events that have happened. This knowledge puts life in perspective.

Get Published, Inc!
Thorofare, NJ 08086
10 March, 2010
BA2010069